How We Make Music

M.L. Robertson

Rourke

Publishing LLC
Vero Beach, Florida 32964

www.rourkepublishing.com

PHOTO CREDITS: © Andrea Gingerich: page 4; © PhotoDisc: page 5; © Christine Nichols: page 6; © Michelle Junior: page 8; © Donald Johansson: pages 9 (top), 10; © Julie Deshales: page 9 (inset); © Galina Barskay: page 11; © Bonnie Jacobs: page 12 (top); © Robert Brown: page 12 (inset); © Noel Dietrich: page 13; © Karla Caspari: page 14 (top); © Anita Patterson: page 14 (inset); © Brad Whitsitt: page 15; © Chris Johnson: page 16; © Ericsphotography: page 17 (top); © Paul Cohen: page 17; © Dale Hogan: page 18 (top); © Digital Archive Japan, Inc: pages 18 (inset), 20 (top), 22; © Francisco Oreleana: page 19; © Jason Lugo: page 20 (inset); © Tom Nguyen: page 21

Editor: Robert Stengard-Olliges

Cover design by Nicola Stratford

Library of Congress Cataloging-in-Publication Data

Robertson, M.L.,
  How we make music / M.L. Robertson.
    p. cm. -- (The world around me)
  Includes index.
  ISBN 1-59515-991-6 (hardcover)
  ISBN 1-59515-962-2 (softcover)

Printed in the USA

CG/CG

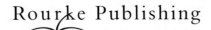

Rourke Publishing

www.rourkepublishing.com – sales@rourkepublishing.com
Post Office Box 3328, Vero Beach, FL 32964

Table of Contents

Introduction

We make music by singing a song. What songs can you sing? Can you sing a song right now?

We make music by playing an **instrument**. Do you play an instrument? Would you like to play an instrument?

The String Family

Instruments that are similar are called a family. The instruments in the string family are usually played by pulling a bow across the strings.

Our fingers change the **pitch** by pressing on the strings. The bow makes the strings vibrate and that makes the sound.

Guitars and banjos are usually played by **plucking** the strings. Which string instrument would you like to play?

The Woodwind Family

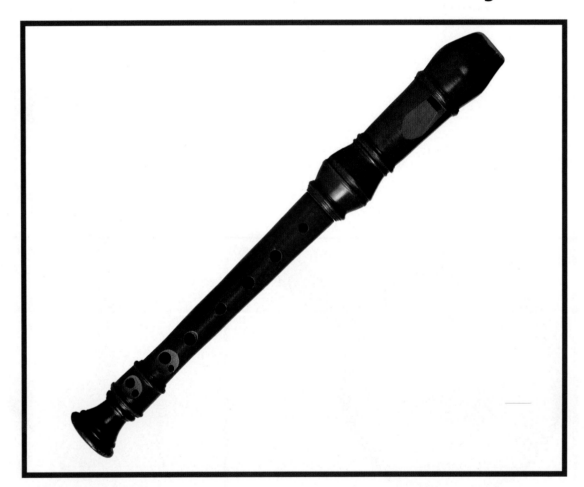

There are many instruments in the woodwind family. They are called woodwinds because at one time they were all made of wood.

Do you ever blow on a bottle to make a sound? That is how we make the sound on a flute.

The woodwind family includes instruments whose mouthpieces use a single **reed**. Clarinets and saxophones use one reed.

The oboe and bassoon are called double reed instruments. A double reed mouthpiece has two reeds tied together.

The Brass Family

Instruments in the brass family are made of **brass**. Sound is made by blowing on a mouthpiece that is shaped like a cup.

The end of the horn is shaped like a bell. We change
the pitch by pressing down on **valves** with our fingers.

Changing the pitch on a trombone is different. The player must move a slide back and forth to change pitch.

The tuba is the biggest brass instrument. A Sousaphone is a tuba we can play while marching

The Percussion Family

Members of this family are called percussion because we strike them in some way to make a sound. Many percussion instruments are used to make **rhythm**.

We shake some percussion instruments to make a sound.

Making Music in Groups

A choir is a group of boys, girls, or boys and girls who sing together. A band is a group of people playing woodwind, brass and percussion instruments together.

A group of people playing instruments together is called an orchestra. Choirs, bands and orchestras all have one thing in common a leader called a **conductor**.

Would you like to sing in a choir? Would you like to play an instrument? Making music is fun. Making music makes other people happy too.

Glossary

brass (BRASS) – a type of metal instruments are made of

conductor (kuhn DUHK tur) – the leader of a choir, orchestra, or band

instrument (IN struh muhnt) – any object used to make music

pitch (PICH) – the highness or lowness of a sound

pluck (PLUHK) – using fingers or a pick to strum the strings of a string instrument like a guitar

reed (REED) – a part of a reed plant used on the mouthpiece of some woodwind instruments to create the sound

rhythm (riTH uhm) – a regular beat

valves (VALVZ) – the part of a brass instrument used to change pitch

Index

Further Reading

Hunka, Alison. *Playing the Violin and Stringed Instruments*. Stargazer Books, 2005.

Lynch, Wendy. *Woodwind*. Heinemann Library, 2002.

Wade-Matthews, Max. *Musical Instruments*. Lorenz, 2003.

Websites To Visit

http://www.playmusic.org/

http://www.sfskids.org/

http://www.nyphilkids.org/

About The Author

Dr. Marvin Robertson spent over 43 years as a music professor/adminstrator and choral director. Though his major responsibilities were on the university level he always found time to work with children in making music. He believes every child has a right to and can benefit from learning music.